GOLDILOCKS
AND THE
THREE BEARS

by Jackie Walter and Lucy Makuc

W
FRANKLIN WATTS
LONDON•SYDNEY

Once upon a time, there were three bears
– Mummy Bear, Daddy Bear and
Baby Bear. They lived in a cottage
deep in the woods.

One morning, Mummy Bear made porridge for breakfast. But it was far too hot to eat.

"Let's go for a walk while the porridge cools down," said Mummy Bear.

So off they went.

A little girl called Goldilocks
came walking through the woods.
She saw the bears' cottage.
"What a pretty cottage," she said.
And she went to have a look.

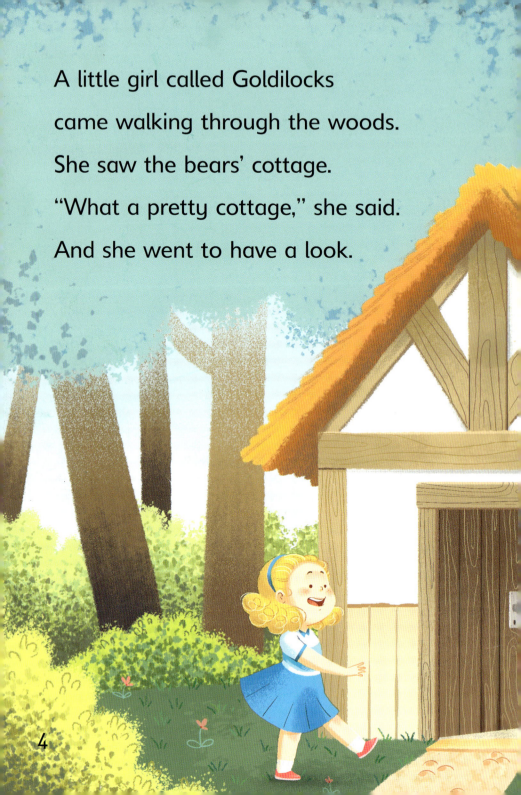

Goldilocks looked through the windows.
She saw the porridge on the table.
"Oh, I'm hungry, and that looks good,"
she cried. "I must try some!"

She walked though the door
and went into the kitchen.

First, Goldilocks tried

Daddy Bear's porridge.

"Ouch, too hot!" she cried.

Next, she tried Mummy Bear's porridge.

"Yuck, too cold!" she cried.

Then she tried Baby Bear's porridge.
"Yum, that's just right!" she said,
and she ate it all up.

Goldilocks went into the sitting room.

She saw three chairs.

First, Goldilocks tried Daddy Bear's chair.

"Ouch, too hard!"

she cried.

Next, she tried Mummy Bear's chair.

"Yuck, too soft!"

she cried.

Then she tried Baby Bear's chair.

"Ah, that's just right!" she said,

and she sat down. But she was too big,

and she broke the chair!

Goldilocks went upstairs. She saw three beds. First, Goldilocks tried Daddy Bear's bed. "Ouch, too hard!" she cried.

Next, she tried Mummy Bear's bed, "Yuck, too soft!" she cried.

Then she tried Baby Bear's bed.
"Oh, that's just right!" she said
and snuggled down for a nap.

The three bears came home from
their walk. They were very surprised
to see their cottage door was wide open.
"Who's been eating my porridge?"
growled Daddy Bear.
"Who's been eating my porridge?"
grumbled Mummy Bear.

"Who's been eating my porridge?"
grizzled Baby Bear. "They've eaten it
all up!"

Next, the three bears looked at their chairs.

"Who's been sitting in my chair?"

growled Daddy Bear.

"Who's been sitting in my chair?"

grumbled Mummy Bear.

"Who's been sitting in my chair?"

grizzled Baby Bear.

"They've broken it!"

17

Then the three bears went upstairs.

"Who's been sleeping in my bed?"

growled Daddy Bear.

"Who's been sleeping in my bed?"

grumbled Mummy Bear.

"Who is sleeping in my bed?"

grizzled Baby Bear.

"It's a horrible little girl!"

Goldilocks woke up with a jump. She saw the three angry bears looking at her. She raced downstairs and out of the door and ran all the way home. The three bears never saw her again.

Story order

Look at these 5 pictures and captions.
Put the pictures in the right order
to retell the story.

1

The Three Bears come back home.

2

Goldilocks breaks a chair.

3

Goldilocks runs away!

4

Goldilocks finds a cottage door open.

5

Goldilocks spots the bowls of porridge.

Independent Reading

This series is designed to provide an opportunity for your child to read on their own. These notes are written for you to help your child choose a book and to read it independently.

In school, your child's teacher will often be using reading books which have been banded to support the process of learning to read. Use the book band colour your child is reading in school to help you make a good choice. *Goldilocks and the Three Bears* is a good choice for children reading at Purple Band in their classroom to read independently.

The aim of independent reading is to read this book with ease, so that your child enjoys the story and relates it to their own experiences.

About the book

In this famous fairy tale, the three bears go out for a walk while their breakfast cools. When they return, they discover Goldilocks has entered their house!

Before reading

Help your child to learn how to make good choices by asking:
"Why did you choose this book? Why do you think you will enjoy it?"
Look at the cover together and ask: "What do you think the story will be about?" Ask your child to think of what they already know about the story context. Then ask your child to read the title aloud.
Ask: "What are the Three Bears doing? What do you think Goldilocks is doing?"
Remind your child that they can sound out the letters to make a word if they get stuck.
Decide together whether your child will read the story independently or read it aloud to you.

During reading

Remind your child of what they know and what they can do independently. If reading aloud, support your child if they hesitate or ask for help by telling the word. If reading to themselves, remind your child that they can come and ask for your help if stuck.

After reading

Support comprehension by asking your child to tell you about the story. Use the story order puzzle to encourage your child to retell the story in the right sequence, in their own words. The correct sequence can be found on the next page.

Help your child think about the messages in the book that go beyond the story and ask: "How do each of the bears feel when they find Goldilocks in their house?"

Give your child a chance to respond to the story: "What was your favourite part and why? What would you do if you found something of yours that had been broken?"

Extending learning

Help your child understand the story structure by using the same sentence patterning and adding different elements. "Let's make up a new story about Goldilocks. What might she find in the woods this time. How could she behave differently?"

In the classroom, your child's teacher may be teaching different kinds of sentences. There are many examples in this book that you could look at with your child, including statements, commands and questions. Find these together and point out how the end punctuation can help us decide what kind of sentence it is.

Franklin Watts
First published in Great Britain in 2022
by The Watts Publishing Group

Series Editors: Jackie Hamley and Melanie Palmer
Series Advisors and Development Editors: Dr Sue Bodman and Glen Franklin
Series Designers: Peter Scoulding and Cathryn Gilbert

A CIP catalogue record for this book is
available from the British Library.

ISBN 978 1 4451 8405 0 (hbk)
ISBN 978 1 4451 8406 7 (pbk)
ISBN 978 1 4451 8466 1 (library ebook)
ISBN 978 1 4451 8465 4 (ebook)

Printed in China

Franklin Watts
An imprint of
Hachette Children's Group
Part of The Watts Publishing Group
Carmelite House
50 Victoria Embankment
London EC4Y 0DZ

An Hachette UK Company
www.hachette.co.uk

www.reading-champion.co.uk

FSC
www.fsc.org
MIX
Paper from
responsible sources
FSC® C104740

Answer to Story order: 4,5,2,1,3